Shutterbug Books
SCIENCE

Changing Seasons

by Elena Martin

STECK-VAUGHN
A Harcourt Company

www.steck-vaughn.com

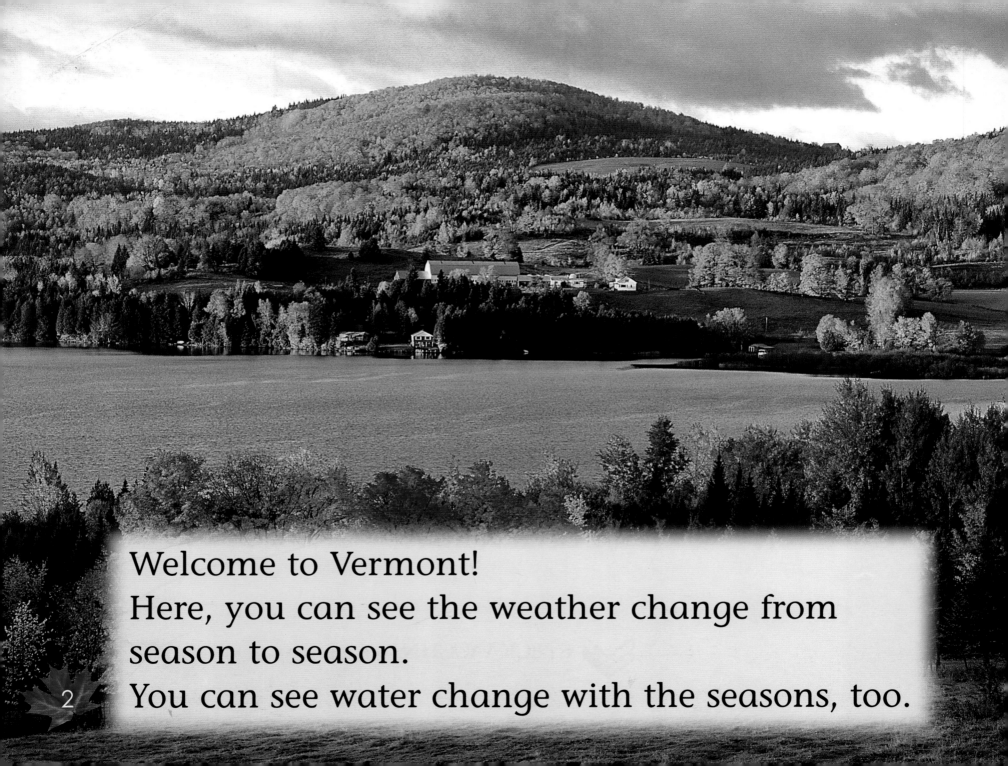

Welcome to Vermont!
Here, you can see the weather change from season to season.
You can see water change with the seasons, too.

Whoooosh! Leaves begin to fall from the trees.
Cool water flows in Vermont's streams.
Fall is the driest season since there is little rain.

3

The air grows cooler.
Frost covers the grass and plants each morning.

4

It's time to pick pumpkins.
Colder weather and a new season are coming.

5

Brrr! Winter is the coldest season. It's time for warm coats and hats.

In Vermont, it gets so cold that lakes freeze.
You can skate on the ice during winter.

7

Even the clouds change in winter.
Clouds are made of tiny drops of water.

The water from clouds changes on cold winter days.
Snow falls instead of rain.

9

10

Drip! Drip! The snow and ice are melting. The days are getting warmer.

Spring has come to Vermont.
Flowers grow and birds build nests.

What else happens in spring?
It rains!

Spring is the rainiest season.
The rain helps plants grow.

Summer comes after the spring.
Summer is the warmest season.
It can get hot.

Splash! It feels good to swim on a hot summer day.
But summer will not last.
What season will come next?

Changing Seasons

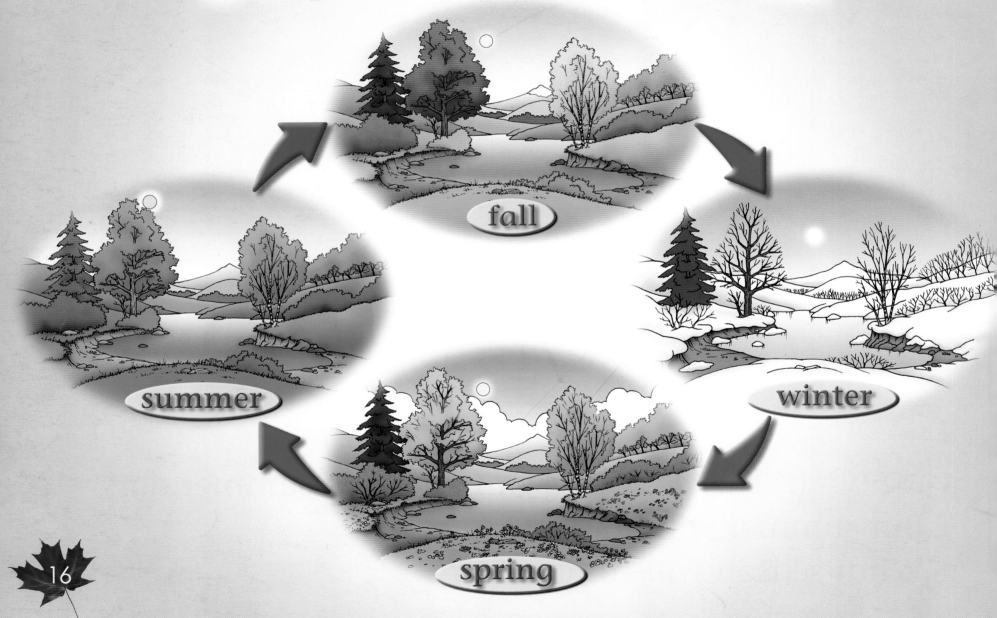

fall

summer

winter

spring

16